I See Purple

Trudy Micco

Bailey Books
an imprint of
Enslow Publishers, Inc.
40 Industrial Road
Box 398
Berkeley Heights, NJ 07922
USA
http://www.enslow.com

Bailey Books, an imprint of Enslow Publishers, Inc.

Copyright © 2011 by Enslow Publishers, Inc.

Library of Congress Cataloging-in-Publication Data

Micco, Trudy.
I see purple / Trudy Micco.
p. cm. — (All about colors)
Summary: "Learn about the color purple"— Provided by publisher.
  Includes bibliographical references and index.
ISBN 978-0-7660-3792-2
1. Purple—Juvenile literature. 2. Color—Juvenile literature. I. Title.
QC495.5.M476 2011
535.6—dc22
                                    2010011884
Paperback ISBN: 978-1-59845-167-2

Printed in the United States of America

062010 Lake Book Manufacturing, Inc., Melrose Park, IL

· 10 9 8 7 6 5 4 3 2 1

Note to Parents and Teachers

Help pre-readers get a jumpstart on reading. These lively stories introduce simple concepts with repetition of words and short simple sentences. Photos and illustrations fill the pages with color and effectively enhance the text. Free Educator Guides are available for this series at www.enslow.com. Search for the *All About Colors* series name.

Contents

Words to Know

cat   **love**   **purple**

I love my purple cat,

in a purple room,

on a purple hat,

in a purple field,

with a purple dog,

by a purple flower,

with a purple bug,

on a purple ball.

I love . . .

my purple cat!

Read More

Gordon, Sharon. *Purple*. New York: Benchmark Books, 2005.

Johnson, Crockett. *Harold and the Purple Crayon*. New York: Harper, 1955.

Web Sites

Enchanted Learning. *I Love Colors: Shades of Purple*.
<http://www.enchantedlearning.com/colors/purple.shtml>

Primary Games. *Colors*.
<http://www.primarygames.com/color_fun/color_fun.htm>

Index

Guided Reading Level: **B**
Guided Reading Leveling System is based on the guidelines
recommended by Fountas and Pinnell.

Word Count: 38